MATH ADVENTURES

BELLA BUILDS A FORT

A MEASURING ADVENTURE

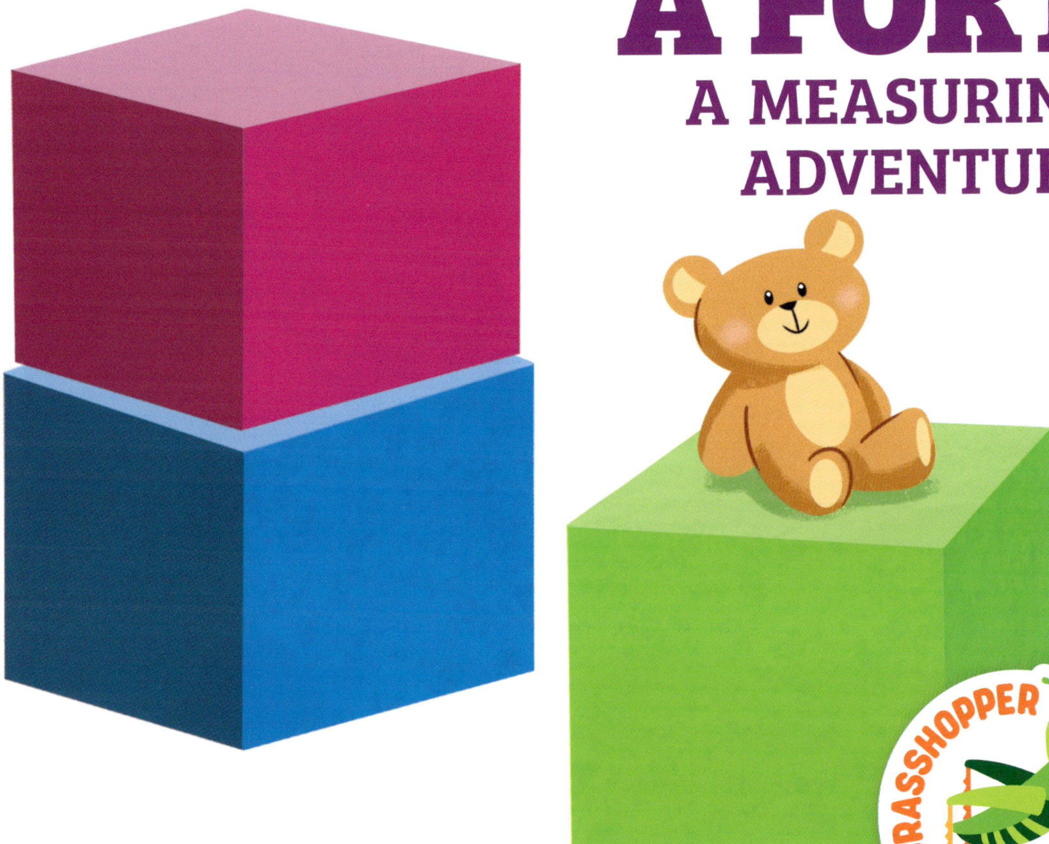

by Elizabeth Everett
illustrated by Amy Zhing

Tools for Parents & Teachers

Grasshopper Books enhance imagination and introduce the earliest readers to fiction with fun storylines and illustrations. The easy-to-read text supports early reading experiences with repetitive sentence patterns and sight words.

Before Reading

- Discuss the cover illustration. What do readers see?
- Look at the picture glossary together. Discuss the words.

Read the Book

- Read the book to the child, or have him or her read independently.
- "Walk" through the book and look at the illustrations. Who is the main character? What is happening in the story?

After Reading

- Prompt the child to think more. Ask: Bella measures and builds a fort using blocks. Have you ever measured something? What was it?

Grasshopper Books are published by Jump!
5357 Penn Avenue South
Minneapolis, MN 55419
www.jumplibrary.com

Library of Congress Cataloging-in-Publication Data

Names: Everett, Elizabeth, author. | Zhing, Amy, illustrator.
Title: Bella builds a fort: a measuring adventure
by Elizabeth Everett; illustrated by Amy Zhing.
Description: Minneapolis, MN: Jump!, Inc., [2023]
Series: Math adventures
Includes index. | Audience: Ages 5–8
Identifiers: LCCN 2021970006 (print)
LCCN 2021058709 (ebook)
ISBN 9781636908618 (hardcover)
ISBN 9781636908625 (paperback)
ISBN 9781636908632 (ebook)
Subjects: LCSH: Measurement—Juvenile literature.
Classification: LCC QA465 .E94 2023 (print)
LCC QA465 (ebook) | DDC 530.8—dc23/eng/20220126
LC record available at https://lccn.loc.gov/2021970006
LC ebook record available at https://lccn.loc.gov/2021970095

Editor: Jenna Gleisner
Direction and Layout: Molly Ballanger
Illustrator: Amy Zhing

Printed in the United States of America at
Corporate Graphics in North Mankato, Minnesota.

Table of Contents

Measuring with Blocks

Bella is excited to go to the playground.

But when she looks outside, it is raining!

I'll build a fort to play in instead, Bella thinks.

She gets her blocks out.

Bella pushes blocks together.

They make a straight line.

She measures it.

The line is six blocks long.

6

She puts three blocks on each end.

Then she fills in the missing blocks to make a rectangle.

The rectangle is four blocks wide.

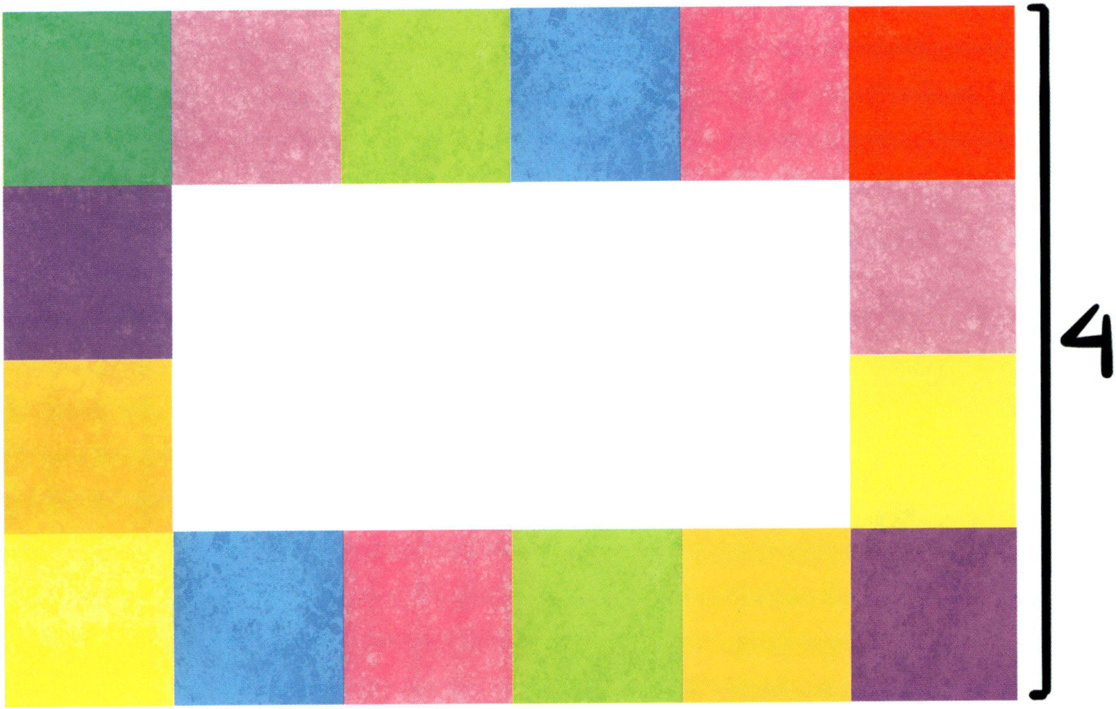

Next, Bella builds the walls.

She stacks blocks on top.

The walls are two blocks high.

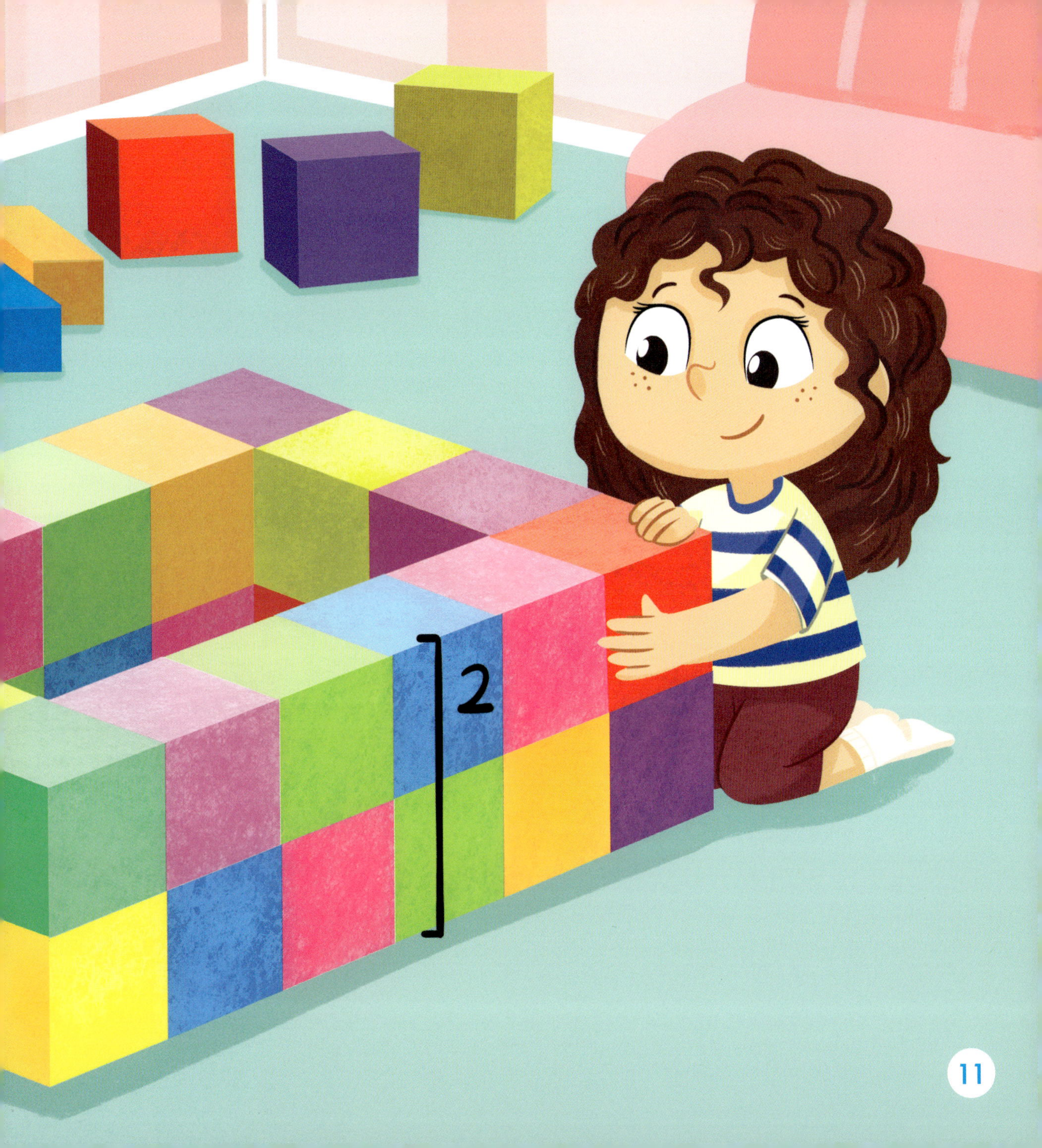
2

Bella's sister comes in.

"What is that?" asks Emma.

"This is a fort we can
play in!" says Bella.
"The length is six blocks.
The width is four blocks.
The height is two blocks."

"Let's make it taller!" says Emma.

"OK!" Bella says. "Let's make it twice as high! Then it will be four blocks tall."

4

"Remember, Emma. The blocks all have to be the same size," Bella says.

“I like building!” says Emma.

"I like measuring!" says Bella.

"All done! Now let's build a tower!" Bella says.

Let's Review!

Bella counts blocks to measure and build a fort. Look at this tower. How many blocks is it long? How many blocks is it wide? How many blocks is it tall?

Let's Review! Answer Key: **length:** 3 **height:** 7 **width:** 3

Picture Glossary

fort
A building with high walls.

height
The measurement of how tall something is.

length
The measurement of something from end to end.

measures
Finds out the particular size of something.

stacks
Sets things on top of one another.

width
The measurement from one side of something to the other.

Index

To Learn More

FACT SURFER

Finding more information is as easy as 1, 2, 3.

1. Go to www.factsurfer.com
2. Enter "**Bellabuildsafort**" into the search box.
3. Choose your book to see a list of websites.